Connie & Sabrina
In Waiting

by Sandra Marie Vago

SAMUEL FRENCH, INC.

45 WEST 25TH STREET   NEW YORK 10010
7623 SUNSET BOULEVARD HOLLYWOOD 90046
LONDON   TORONTO

Copyright © 1989, 1994 by Sandra Marie Vago

To my father, Hal.

IMPORTANT BILLING AND CREDIT
REQUIREMENTS

The original St. Louis workshop of *Connie and Sabrina In Waiting* was produced at the Kirkwood Theatre, St. Louis, Missouri, by Black Box Productions. It was directed by Sandra Marie Vago and had the following cast:

SABRINA	Jane Squier
CONNIE	Mary Knoll
MICHAEL	Jeffrey Roberts
FUNERAL ATTENDANT	
PRINCIPAL	
JERRY	
DR. HAUSLER	Greg Hunsaker
DUGGIE	
DOUGLAS	
NURSE	
DR. MACON	
NURSE	Teresa Farraro
CARRIE	
MOTHER	

Lights and Production: Jim Davis
Sound Design: Joseph Rodriguez
Properties & Set Design: Sally David

CHARACTERS

SABRINA — a woman in her mid-to-late fifties.

CONNIE — her friend, goes from 16 to fifties.

MICHAEL — Sabrina's husband, goes from 16 to fifties.

<table>
<tr><td>Funeral Attendant
Principal
Jerry
Dr. Hausler
Duggie
Douglas</td><td>Can be played by one actor</td></tr>
</table>

<table>
<tr><td>Nurse
Dr. Macon
Nurse
Carrie
Mother</td><td>Can be played by one actor</td></tr>
</table>

TIME & PLACE

Early fifties through 1994.

CONNIE & SABRINA
IN WAITING

Scene 1

SCENE: A simple wooden coffin sits upstage center with a single chair and dim SPOTLIGHT. There is one bouquet of flowers next to the coffin. Stage left is a waiting room setting. It could be any waiting room, any time, depending upon the simple change of some properties and the addition or deletion of a set piece or two. Stage right, same, so that "memory" scenes take place in front and on either side of "funeral parlor." In the first memory scene, the set is of that ominous waiting room outside the high school principal's office. Only the coffin area is lighted at rise.

AT RISE: MUSIC generally played in funeral parlors begins to come up softly as we see a WOMAN enter. SHE's dressed as if going to a party and carries a single yellow rose, a portable record player and a Dean Martin record album and in her straw bag, SHE has a red and white checkered tablecloth. SHE throws the tablecloth over the coffin and sets the wine and album up on it, then stands back, suddenly perturbed by the whole thing.

SABRINA. I must admit, you've had some hair-brained schemes in your day, Con, a few real humdingers when it comes to canceling on me! One, that comes flashing vividly into mind, being the time you let me wait sixteen hours at the airport. You remember, the time you cooked up that elaborate story about being high-jacked! What really happened was you met some sandal salesman in Cozumel who looked like Desi Arnaz and fell madly in love, for the afternoon! ... Oh, but this, this my dearest, bestest friend, is the coup de grace! ...

You knew I'd refuse to hear any more phoney excuses, any more cancellations. You knew I would not take your standing me up, sitting down! You knew I would never, I repeat, *never* speak to you again if you did this to me one more time ... And dammit, you found a way to do it anyhow! (*SHE Stops, touches the coffin, takes out a hanky and blows her nose and then goes on.*) Damn it, Con. You crazy broad. You can't just die on me ... not just like that ... not without telling me. You never tell me anything!!

ATTENDANT. (*Enters*) Good evening.

SABRINA. Depends on who you're talking to. I suppose if we took a vote right this minute, it'd surely be a deadlock.

ATTENDANT. I beg your pardon?

SABRINA. Forget it. This is Madeline Bartoli? I had this message on my machine. A man, but then it would've been, said she'd asked him to call me, tell me where she'd be, why she didn't show ... Oh, god, this is so bizarre. (*SHE sits down.*)

ATTENDANT. One moment ... (*HE checks a tag at the end of the coffin.*) Tag says Madeline Bartoli.

SABRINA. Tag! That's Connie. I never could go anywhere with her when she didn't have some damned tag hangin' on her. (*SHE giggles.*) Say, mister, that tag doesn't by any chance have a red, blue or green dot ...

ATTENDANT. Excuse me?!

SABRINA. No, I don't suppose Ralph Lauren makes coffins. And if he did, they wouldn't be reduced.

ATTENDANT. Well, if there's nothing more ... I'm just about to start a service for a group down the hall.

SABRINA. You go ahead, she and I have lots to talk about.

ATTENDANT. Well, there's coffee down the hall.

SABRINA. Thanks, but caffeine makes me crazy.

(*HE looks at her, rather puzzled, then nods and leaves.*)

SABRINA. Could use a scotch, though. Don't suppose there's a bar in this joint ... Hell've a way to hear about this, Con ... a message on my machine. (*SHE goes to the coffin.*) So much for promises. You gave me your solemn word this time. "No way I'm missin' this dinner date, Brina," that's what you said. "It's been twenty-five years since we ate spaghetti and drank Blue Nun at Jimmy B's. I'm just dyin' to see if Stanley still has any of that beautiful curly hair!" ... Sure, just dyin' ... I meant it, Con, when I said I wouldn't stand for any more phoney excuses. Standin' me up again! (*Pause*) Connie Ann Louisa Maria ... (*SHE chuckles to herself at the pet name.*) Dyin' to find out about Stanley's hair, huh? Couldn't wait to have a plate of spaghetti, huh? You have any idea how long I waited at that bar?! You know how many glasses of Blue Nun I hadda drink? ... Oh, and the spaghetti, I not only ate both plates, with meatballs, but I forced down two orders of cheese garlic bread ... just for you! Just 'cause I knew you'd order it for us ... I don't even like cheese garlic bread! (*Pause*.) He's losin' most of it ... Stanley. Everybody was sorry they missed you. Binky played that damned "Volare" a hunnerd and fifty-seven times and Jimmy B played "That's Amore," just for you. You shoulda been there. The whole place chimed in on, "when the moon hit'sa your eye like a bigga pizza pie" ... even me. (*SHE laughs*.) Okay, I know, so I can't sing. So we all got our own kinda hell ... Oops, sorry. I mean not that I think for one minute that that's where a very old but unreliable friend of mine mighta made a pit stop, but it's not a word I should use loosely, under the circumstances. After all, we were never what could've been even remotely misconstrued as angelic material. (*Pause*.) You were, after all, always getting me into trouble. Even from the beginning outside Mr. Hornsby's office.

(As the LIGHTS dim on the coffin and come up on the waiting room, a YOUNG WOMAN sits fidgeting. SABRINA, still as she was in the beginning but gone back in memory, appears.)

CONNIE. Hi. What ya in for?
SABRINA. In for?
CONNIE. Your crime, dastardly deed, You know?
SABRINA. Oh. Nothing. I'm not "in" ... at least not yet. I'm enrolling.
CONNIE. (*Very serious*.) Oh. My condolences.
SABRINA. Thanks.

CONNIE. So what'd ya do that made 'em send ya to Sing Sing?

SABRINA. I moved into the neighborhood.

CONNIE. That'll do it.

SABRINA. What're you in for?

CONNIE. Disrupting Pedigre's class. (*SHE pulls a frog out and pets it.*)

SABRINA. Pedigre?

CONNIE. Yeah, what a joke. He does not have a drop, trust me!

SABRINA. Oh, I do.

CONNIE. What's your name?

SABRINA. Wanda Goodman.

CONNIE. Yuk!

SABRINA. Thanks!

CONNIE. No ... listen, you know who you look like?

SABRINA. (*A bit perplexed.*) No. Who?

CONNIE. D'you see the movie where Audrey Hepburn played this girl named Sabrina?

SABRINA. No. I didn't see it. You think I look like Audrey Hepburn?

CONNIE. No. Sabrina. That's such a cool name, but it doesn't look right on me.

SABRINA. You mean sound right.

CONNIE. Look right! I don't have the right look.

SABRINA. (*Takes the frog.*) Can I hold him?

CONNIE. (*Impressed because she's not afraid.*) Sure. Just be careful.

SABRINA. That is a cool name. I hate Wanda.

CONNIE. So, call yourself, Sabrina. Sabrina Anna Louisa Maria ... (*SHE laughs and the door opens. MR. HORNSBY enters.*) The warden.

MR. HORNSBY. Madeline. I see you're visiting me again. (*To Sabrina*) I'll be with you in a minute, miss ...
SABRINA. Goodman, sir. Sabrina Goodman.

(*HE looks down at his file and the FROG croaks as SHE coughs.*)

MR. HORNSBY. I have "Wanda" ... Are you all right?
SABRINA. Fine. I, uh, I go by my middle name.
MR. HORNSBY. All right. Now, Madeline. What's this about refusing to dissect a frog in biology class?

(*The FROG croaks and again, SABRINA coughs.*)

SABRINA. Sorry. Does Mr. Pedigre teach biology?
CONNIE. Yep. Can you stand it?! (*SHE bursts into laughter.*)
MR. HORNSBY. I asked you a question, young lady.
CONNIE. First of all, sir, it wasn't dead, the frog. It hopped out of the jar of its own accord. I mean it wasn't even sleepy!
MR. HORNSBY. You're supposed to use chloroform, Madeline. Mr. Pedigre says you didn't want to chloroform the frog.
CONNIE. How'd you like it if somebody you trusted chloroformed you and then dissected you when you weren't looking?
MR. HORNSBY. That's what frogs are for, Madeline.
CONNIE. Well, not if you ask the frogs.
MR. HORNSBY. How do you expect to learn about biology if you don't dissect the frog?

CONNIE. I don't honestly see what importance this whole thing bares on my future as a rock 'n roll singer, Mr. Hornsby.

MR. HORNSBY. You're not a rock 'n roll singer now. You're a student.

CONNIE. But when I'm an adult, I don't think I need to know all that if I'm gonna be a singer's what I'm saying ... It bears no importance on my future as an adult, but it certainly makes a difference to the frog!

MR. HORNSBY. I don't intend to argue, young lady. Biology is required.

CONNIE. Yes, sir, but I thought we'd be studying plants.

SABRINA. I think that's Botany.

CONNIE. Oh, well that explains it!

MR. HORNSBY. I don't have time for this.... Right now I need to get Wanda ...

SABRINA. Sabrina, sir.

MR. HORNSBY. Well please change it on your records.... If you have your class schedule, I suggest you get right to your class. Do you have a question?

SABRINA. Only that, well, I'm taking biology and I thought maybe Madeline and I ...

CONNIE. Connie.

SABRINA. Excuse me?

CONNIE. Connie, as in Connie Francis. *Where the Boys Are*, did you see that movie?

SABRINA. I saw that one.

CONNIE. I look just like her in that movie.

SABRINA. Oh, yeah. You do look like ...

MR. HORNSBY. Girls!!

SABRINA. Oh, sorry. I just meant that maybe we could be partners, Connie and I. We had partners in my last school in biology.

CONNIE. We do here, too. Mine's James Reddig, he's an asshole.

MR. HORNSBY. That is enough!

CONNIE. Well, he is, ask anybody.

MR. HORNSBY. Please go and take this up with Mr. Pedigre. Madeline, no more problems, you understand?

(There's a KNOCK at his door.)

MR. HORNSBY. Excuse me. (*HE exits.*)

SABRINA. Connie, that's perfect for you. You really do look like her in that movie ... wow, it was great!

(Taking the cue, CONNIE starts singing loudly from the movie. SHE stops, seeing something. Then pulls a tag off her sweater.)

CONNIE. Hey, you wanna go shopping after school? My mom works at Marks Department Store. They don't have the really neat designer stuff but it's passable. One of these days I'm goin' to New York where the really neat stuff is ... of course, I'll buy it on sale. Nobody should ever pay retail you know, that's dumb. Your mom work?

SABRINA. No. She's crippled, she has to stay in a wheelchair.

CONNIE. What happened to her?

SABRINA. No. She's always been like that.

CONNIE. No kidding? How'd she have you, I mean if she was crippled?

SABRINA. How you think? Same way she had my sisters and my little brother ... or, don't you know?

CONNIE. Of course I know. I'm studying biology, remember?

CONNIE. So, what's your dad?

SABRINA. Whatta you mean, what is he?

CONNIE. What's he do?

SABRINA. He's a shoe salesman. Athletic shoes. 'Course, he doesn't make a much money off my mom!

(THEY both look at one another for a second and then begin to laugh.)

SABRINA. So what's your dad?

CONNIE. He doesn't work. He's a writer.... Actually I think he's a writer, I don't see him much. He stays locked in this attic room. My mom slides messages and food under the door to 'im and we hear this occasional tap tap tapping. That's how we know he's still alive.

SABRINA. I don't know how I'd find out if mine's still alive. He left a few years ago. My mom says he couldn't sell many shoes to anybody else either. He may not be a salesman anymore, who knows?

CONNIE. Holy cow, we do have a lot in common.

SABRINA. We do?

CONNIE. Yeah! It's been a long time since my dad came out of the attic. He may not be a writer anymore, who knows?!

SABRINA. You're crazy!

CONNIE. So, when we get to Pedigre's class lemme do the talking. He's totally zonkers! Sixty five if he's a day, Wears these little round glasses and has three, maybe four white hairs that stick straight up outta the top of his head. But he thinks he's a ladies' man. He only sent me to the office 'cause he's not gettin' anywhere. He lovvvves blondes!... Wait'll he gets a load of you. He'll flip!

SABRINA. I can't tell you how happy that makes me.

CONNIE. I'm hip. Wanna come over after school?

SABRINA. Sorry, I can't. I have to help my mom.

CONNIE. So I'll come help you.

SABRINA. No thanks.

CONNIE. We can't be best friends if we don't help each other for crimony sakes!

SABRINA. I don't need any help.

CONNIE. So we'll try it on a trial basis. Uh, oh ... here he comes.

SABRINA. Here "who" comes?

CONNIE. Michael, a friend of mine. He can smell a new girl a mile away. Especially if she's cute.

MICHAEL. (*Entering*) Hey, Madeline, what's up? Who's your friend?

CONNIE. I refuse to answer anyone who disregards my wishes to be called by my chosen name and instead insists on calling by one in which I had no consultation. Ignore him, Sabrina.

MICHAEL. Sabrina. Hi, I'm Michael.

SABRINA. I don't hear a thing, do you?

CONNIE. Nope.

MICHAEL. Okay, Connie Francis, introduce me.

CONNIE. Connie will do, thank you, Wally.

SABRINA. Wally? You mean he has one too?

MICHAEL. Don't even think about it!

CONNIE. Okay. Michael Roberts, this is Sabrina Goodman. (*SHE whispers to Sabrina.*) But he looks just like Wally Cox in Mr. Peepers!

(*The GIRLS giggle.*)

SABRINA. I think I'm beginning to make out a faint figure. Hello, Michael.
MICHAEL. Something tells me I'm in trouble already. Especially if your name is from that movie.
CONNIE. He loves me, he just won't admit it. Hey, Mikey, whyn't ya ask Sabrina with us to the show, Saturday?... You can get out for that, can't ya, Brin?
SABRINA. I don't ...
MICHAEL. Sure, wanna come?
CONNIE. Mikey's an usher. He gets us in the side door, free.
MICHAEL. I do as long as you keep your big mouth shut.
SABRINA. Oh. I wouldn't wanna ...
MICHAEL. I didn't mean to you ... it's okay if she tells you.
SABRINA. Well, I don't ...
MICHAEL. Good, great! I'll see you guys Saturday. Miss Francis will show you the side door. 7:15. (*HE starts out and then stops.*) Please, tell me you're not as crazy as she is. (*HE lovingly and playfully squeezes Connie and tossles her hair.*) One Connie Francis is enough for any man.

(*LIGHTS fade on the three of them.*
LIGHTS come up again on Sabrina at the coffin.)

SABRINA. Michael always did say you were too much for one man. He was right. Lot's of people thought you were crazy. They thought we both were ... (*SHE laughs*.) You were determined to get the two of us together. Funny. I honestly thought it was you he liked. I even felt bad when he asked me out, I thought it hurt you. But you either put up one hell've a front or you really did want me and him together. You were determined and you certainly were a pushy broad. I couldn't have missed the movie that Saturday night if I'd wanted to ... God, those were the good years at Sing Sing High. We actually made it to senior year!... There you were, six thousand guys asking you out but all you did that summer was hang out with me and Michael and wait for Duggie to come home. I remember how excited you were when his "boot" was over and you had one whole weekend before he got shipped out. You know, he's the only guy you never associated with some movie star, although you did compare him to a few other notable men.

(LIGHTS come up at the train station waiting room as CONNIE and SABRINA wait for Duggie.)

CONNIE. Do you see him yet?
SABRINA. I've never met him, I don't know what he looks like.
CONNIE. He's like a Greek God! Like Hercules or Adonis. He's ... he's here!

(SHE jumps up and down grabbing Sabrina and the TWO of them jump up and down. A young MAN enters. HE

looks rather ordinary but is wearing a U.S. Army uniform.)

DUGGIE. Sunshine! God, it's good to see you. (*HE picks her up and twirls her, dropping his duffel bag and kissing her. Then to Sabrina:)* Hi. I'm Duggie. (*HE kisses her on the cheek and is quite charming.)*
SABRINA. Hi. I thought you might be.
CONNIE. We have the whole weekend. My parents went away for the weekend and I'm staying with Brin.
DUGGIE. So why are we wasting time?

(HE gives CONNIE several passionate kisses as SABRINA watches, uncomfortable.)

DUGGIE. I'll drop my bag in a locker and we're off. I have so much to tell you ... Oh, Brin? You wanna come with us?
SABRINA. Excuse me?! Uh, no, I don't think so. Michael's picking me up in front. You two go ahead ... You will call me, right?
CONNIE. Cross my heart.
SABRINA. Ah ha.

(LIGHTS dim on them all as THEY leave except for SABRINA who is suddenly turned around by Connie's MOTHER who paces nervously downstage with phone in hand..)

SABRINA. I had to cover for you so much that I kept checking the mirror to see if my nose was growing.
MOTHER. Wanda, where's Connie?

SABRINA. Uh, she, uh … she and Michael went to pick up some things for my mother … at the store.

MOTHER. This is the third time I called. Is that girl doing something she's not supposed to be doing?

SABRINA. Probably.

MOTHER What?!

SABRINA. Probably not … I mean, no, mam. She's fine, honest, I wouldn't lie about that. (*SABRINA feels her nose to see if it's growing.*) Oh, thank God.

MOTHER. What … I can't understand you girls half the time. Tell that daughter of mine we'll be home in the morning. I'll talk to her then … oh, thank you. (*SHE disappears as LIGHTS dim.*)

SABRINA. (*Alone.*) I still don't know how we pulled that one off.

(*LIGHTS come up again as CONNIE and DUGGIE re-enter.*)

SABRINA. Listen, I can wait outside while you two say goodbye.

CONNIE. No, stay.

DUGGIE. We aren't sayin' goodbye. (*HE kisses CONNIE and hugs SABRINA.*) Take care 'a my girl 'til I get back, okay? (*HE takes a high school ring from his finger and gives it to Connie.*) This'll have to do for now. We'll trade it in when I get back.

CONNIE. Duggie's gonna be one one of the first advisors in … where is it?

DUGGIE. Vietnam. I'll be home on leave for Christmas, don't forget. Then, if you're a good girl, maybe I'll have a surprise … Love ya. (*HE kisses her again.*)

CONNIE. Me too, you.

(HE picks up his duffel and starts out.)

DUGGIE. Don't let it rain on ya, sunshine!

(HE exits.)

SABRINA. Good ...
CONNIE. *(Slapping her hand over her mouth.)* No goodbyes, Brina ... we promised.

(THEY watch a minute as HE leaves.)

CONNIE. He didn't make love to me. I wanted him to but he didn't. I begged him to, but he didn't.
SABRINA. You begged him to make love to you?
CONNIE. Yes. I think I'm a sex maniac.
SABRINA. No.
CONNIE. I do. I ... I never felt like that in my entire life. Every time he touched me I thought about reading *Lady Chatterley's Lover*.
SABRINA. No.
CONNIE. Yes ... But you know what?
SABRINA. What?
CONNIE. I also think I love him.
SABRINA. You do?
CONNIE. I guess that's the same way you feel about Michael, huh?
SABRINA. *(Hesitating a moment.)* Sure, I guess.

CONNIE. I'm goin' home now. I'm gonna play "Love Me Tender" all night long. Wanna stop over after the show?

SABRINA. Sure.

CONNIE. (*Dreamily, as SHE leaves.*) Okayyyyy.... See ya later.

(*SABRINA watches as she leaves and MICHAEL enters.*)

MICHAEL. Where is everybody?

SABRINA. Duggie left and Con went home to play "Love Me Tender" all night long. I told her I'd come by after the show.

MICHAEL. I wanted to tell Duggie goodbye.

SABRINA. No "goodbyes," they promised.

MICHAEL. Oh. Did you tell Con about us?

SABRINA. I'll tell her tonight when I go over there.

(*HE smiles and kisses her forehead.*)

SABRINA. I think she loves him ... I love you, Michael.

(*THEY disappear as the LIGHTS go down and come up again on the coffin.*)

SABRINA. "Don't let it rain on ya, sunshine," that's how he'd signed that last letter, Duggie. You must have read it to me a hundred times. Seventeen! That was too young to die. For him *and* for you. (*Pause.*) You never mentioned him again after that summer. I knew things weren't really ever gonna be the same after that. Especially when you met Roger! Good ole Roger! Connie, Sabrina, Roger and Mr. Peepers … incidentally, it's a good thing that one didn't stick, the "Mr. Peeper," I mean. Michael almost killed you for that one, especially when the kids at the show picked up on it. (*SHE laughs.*) He did look like him, though, he still does. (*SHE sits down next to the coffin.*) Oh, Lord, I can still remember hearing the two of you argue about Roger the dodger and "Mr. Peepers," outside the delivery room before Carrie was born. He was so mad at you.

(*LIGHTS fades and come up on MICHAEL and CONNIE in the hospital waiting room. There is a TV also here.*)

MICHAEL. Yeah, well … well, just don't ever call me that in front of anybody again, will ya?
CONNIE. Okay, Peep, I promise.
MICHAEL. That's not funny! And while we're discussing things that are not funny, what was the comedy routine you pulled at the Justice of the Peace with Mr. Most Unlikely?
CONNIE. I feel certain you're not referring to my new husband, Roger.
MICHAEL. Really dumb! Just because me and Brina got married did not mean you hadda run out and do the same thing.
CONNIE. I didn't marry him because of you and Brina. I married him because he joined the Army.
MICHAEL. Oh. Now that clears it all up.
CONNIE. I didn't mean … see what you did, you got me all mixed up. I'm tryin' to watch this show. (*SHE pulls her chair in front of the set.*)

MICHAEL. I can't take this waiting.

CONNIE. Relax. Justine and Bob are bound to win, they're the best dancers.

MICHAEL. I'm not talking about Justine and Bob. I'm talking about Brin. She's been in there for over four hours. Nothing should take four hours!

CONNIE. She's fine. Oh, look at that, would you just look? They are definitely the best couple on the floor. He is so Cocka Moose!

MICHAEL. (*Looking now at the TV.*) Yeah, well Justine's pretty Cocka Meese, herself.

CONNIE. Eh, she's okay … would you sit down!

MICHAEL. (*HE is pacing back and forth.*) I'm tellin' ya, something's wrong. It can't possibly take four hours to have a baby!

CONNIE. Oh? My little nephew was in there twenty-seven hours before he decided to show his demonic little face.

MICHAEL. Twenty-seven hours!?

CONNIE. That's why he's an only child.

MICHAEL. Why did I ask?

CONNIE. Relax, Mikey. Brina's the one on the short end of this stick. She's missin' the most important part of the contest. She sent in five votes for Bob … uh, Justine, herself.

MICHAEL. Tell me somethin', will ya, and don't lie to me?

CONNIE. Uh, oh. Is this gonna be a serious question? You know I hate serious questions, Michael.

MICHAEL. She is, isn't she? Getting the short end of the stick.

CONNIE. Brina? Hell no. She's in there havin' a ball.

MICHAEL. Come on, Madeline.

CONNIE. Dirty pool!

MICHAEL. She married me just to keep me from going overseas, didn't she?

CONNIE. You mean they're not sending guys with glasses and flat feet who have a wife and kid overseas?

MICHAEL. Damn it, Madeline, I'm serious.

CONNIE. Not once but twice, that's twice in one minute he calls me … (*SHE sees he isn't playing.*) She is my best friend in the whole world, okay? She tells me everything. And, she said … oh, I'm not sure I should do this … I'm not sure I can say it …

MICHAEL. I knew it.

CONNIE. She said she loves you, Dummy. And besides, who else would take pity on and marry a guy who looks like Wally Cox?

(*HE throws a magazine at her.*)

CONNIE. Look! Oh, man, you made me miss the spotlight dance. Poor Brina. Here it is just minutes away from the winners being announced and she's in there all alone, pushing and shoving and shoving and push … uh, oh … (*SHE suddenly runs out of the room and we hear her being sick outside. Then SHE returns.*) D'I miss anything?

MICHAEL. You don't look so good. You okay?

CONNIE. I'm fine. It's that big plant next to the elevator that's in trouble.

MICHAEL. Aren't you supposed to be in class or something?

CONNIE. Yeah, yeah. It's only Pedigre, he's used to it.

MICHAEL. I guess Brina told you, we're going to Oklahoma. That's where I got stationed.

CONNIE. Yeah. I think we'll be in Georgia somewhere. I wish we were closer.

MICHAEL. I hear you're getting *closer* to flunking out. You'd better get back to class.

CONNIE. Doesn't matter. I'm quitting.

MICHAEL. I thought you were gonna graduate. Did Roger ...

CONNIE. No. It's my own choice. I've decided to go with him right away.

MICHAEL. Then I suggest you tell your parents you're married. They just might wonder where you went.

CONNIE. I will.

MICHAEL. When?

CONNIE. I'm a little nervous. I mean, my dad may even come out of the attic for this one!

MICHAEL. Don't worry, they can't do more than kill you.

CONNIE. Thanks. Listen, I thought that maybe, my two best friends in the whole world ... my two very best friends might ...

MICHAEL. I am not going with you to tell your parents you ran away and married Roger the dodger.

CONNIE. Please, please, pretty please!

MICHAEL. No. You have to do this yourself. I mean...

(A NURSE enters.)

MICHAEL. Oh my God. What'd I have? Is it a boy or a girl?

CONNIE. Am I an aunt or an uncle?

NURSE. I don't know yet what you had. I just came out to give you both a message.

MICHAEL. Oh.

NURSE. She said, "Michael, relax and stop making Connie crazy." ... Is that you?

CONNIE. Yes. (*To Michael.*) ... Nah nah, nin nah nah!

NURSE. And she said you should go back to class before Mr. Pedigre sends you to the office again for skipping biology. Is your biology teacher really named Mr. Pedigree?

CONNIE. He hasn't got a drop, trust me

NURSE. Well, I suggest you both take her advice. (*SHE exits.*)

MICHAEL. Okay. I'm going back in there. You go back to school. I'll call you when it's over. (*HE starts out.*)

CONNIE. You go ahead. I'll just sit here and wait. I can't leave now, not until I know if I'm an uncle or an aunt. I mean, I can't go in but I want her to know I'm out here ... tell 'er I'll be right here, okay? ... tell 'er ...

MICHAEL. Is this gonna be a long speech? I'll have to tune in for the second half when I get back. (*HE exits.*)

CONNIE. Oh, God. What am I gonna do? How 'm I gonna tell 'em, my mom and dad ... how 'm I gonna tell 'em I'm married and I'm gonna have a baby? They don't even know I smoke!

(*LIGHTS fade on Connie and come up again at the coffin.*)

SABRINA. Well, you managed to talk us into that one. Michael wanted to kill me for making him take us to tell your mom and dad. Roger, dodged that one too. I'll never forget the terror in Michael's eyes when your mother chased you with that baseball bat and he couldn't get the car started. He thought sure it was all over but the Novenas. He never did tell you but it cost us twenty-three dollars to replace the birdbath in your neighbor's yard. (*SHE laughs.*) I guess I shouldn't laugh, it wasn't funny back then. I mean both of us becoming mothers and the year before we'd never even "done it."

SABRINA. You know I was all ready to chew you out last night. You cancelled so many dates these past few years. Always something catastrophic. I remember how you promised we'd keep in touch, the day you left. I was so lonely, you in one Army camp, me in the other, half the country between us. We were separated such a long time ... then, there we were, after your divorce, or I should say before your wedding! ...

(Her LIGHT fades and comes up again on the waiting room. This time it is a wedding chapel. SABRINA is pacing.)

CONNIE. You're making me nervous, will you sit down!?

SABRINA. I can't believe you're gonna do this ... marry this ... this ...

CONNIE. Jerry.

SABRINA. Whoever. You don't show up at the barbecue, Michael's birthday party, and don't even tell us you're getting divorced, and then ...

CONNIE. I couldn't be two places at once.

MICHAEL. It's okay, I understand.

SABRINA. She was getting divorced during your birthday party!

CONNIE. I didn't plan it that way.

SABRINA. You didn't even ask me to be there with you. Michael's birthday!

CONNIE. I didn't wanna spoil the party. It was no big deal.

SABRINA. No big deal?! ... I know you weren't happy with ... Roger. You just got outta that one and now you ask me to meet you here and be your maid of honor while you marry ...

CONNIE. Jerry.

SABRINA. Whoever. It's stupid. Just stupid. You just got out of one. You have a chance to start over.

CONNIE. I am.

MICHAEL. Wait a minute, Brina. Is that what she should do or is it you we're talking about?

SABRINA. Don't be silly, Michael.

CONNIE. No fair fighting on my wedding day.

SABRINA. Is it legal to get married the day after you get divorced?

CONNIE. In another state. We crossed the state line.

MICHAEL. She's just upset about the baby.

CONNIE. What's wrong with the baby?

MICHAEL. Nothing ... I mean ...

SABRINA. What he means is, I'm having another one.

CONNIE. (*Excited.*) Sabrina Louisa Maria Sophia, you little sex maniac! Congratulations.

SABRINA. My name today is Wanda.

CONNIE. Nothing could be that bad. (*SHE laughs and hugs her.*)

MICHAEL. Personally I'm happy as hell. Maybe I'll have my boy this time.

SABRINA. "You" didn't have your girl the last time!

MICHAEL. I'm going outside for a smoke. If Jerry Lee Lewis shows up for this joyous occasion, call me.

CONNIE. Jerry Lee Lewis?! Cute, Michael. If I were going to give him a name it would be Elvis ... from Kid Gallahad. He ...

SABRINA and MICHAEL. (*Chiming in.*) Looks just like him in that movie!!

(THEY all start to laugh.)

CONNIE. He does.

SABRINA. Michael, I'm sorry. I am happy about the baby, honest.

CONNIE. Well.

SABRINA. You can't really wanna marry this guy. He's a musician and he's leaving the country to live in Canada.

CONNIE. He doesn't believe in the war, neither do I. Besides, I'm gonna be the lead singer in his band.

SABRINA. You know nothing about him, and please take note, I did not mention the fact that you can't sing.

CONNIE. Lots of rock 'n roll stars can't sing! Look, Wanda ... you sure you want me to call you that?

SABRINA. Yes.

CONNIE. Okay. I knew Roger for years, we grew up together even if I didn't really date him until after ... anyway, what good did that do me? He beat me up every time he got drunk and he was awful to Mickey.

SABRINA. I didn't mean you should stay with Roger, he was a jerk, we always said that. He wasn't even a good...

CONNIE. Michael are you gonna let her use the "F" word?

SABRINA. *LAY*, for Pete's sake!

CONNIE. She cleaned it up.

MICHAEL. He was an asshole. I told you that before and after you ran away with him. But, and this is a very big "but" ... he looked just like Troy Donahue in that movie!!

CONNIE. He really did. (*SHE laughs.*)

SABRINA. This isn't funny. You don't keep marrying people because they look like Troy Donahue or Elvis Presley.

CONNIE. That was a joke.

SABRINA. You're telling me! ... Looks are not everything. Michael and I have always been very happy.

MOTHER. Thanks a lot.

SABRINA. I didn't mean it that.

CONNIE. Okay, hold it. Why can't we just make this a happy day and stop all this fighting? I assure you I am not marrying Jerry because of his looks.

(*JERRY enters and looks just like Elvis Presley.*)

CONNIE. Well, not totally.

JERRY. Hi, darlin'. (*Imitating Elvis, HE starts to sing, badly, to a rock 'n' roll song, pounding the guitar and singing off-key. As HE finishes, HE twirls the guitar, laughs and twirls Connie.*)

SABRINA. He does *look* like him.

JERRY. D'I miss somethin'?

MOTHER. Probably not. I'm Michael Roberts and this is my wife ... Wanda.

JERRY. Peace, man. Honey, I thought you said your friend Sabrina was comin'?

CONNIE. She couldn't make it.

JERRY. (*To Michael.*) Sorry I'm late ole man. Hope I didn't keep you all waitin' too long.

MICHAEL. No, ole man, just long enough.

JERRY. Huh?

CONNIE. We're next, he means we're next.

JERRY. Hadda go by the pawn shop and pick up my guitar. Connie tell you folks I play and sing a little?

SABRINA. Very little, yes.

CONNIE. He's very good and he's got a band in Ontario waiting for us.

JERRY. Yeah. I already got us booked in a country-western place up there. The Pig's Tail. Con's gonna be a back-up singer.

CONNIE. Back-up?

SABRINA. How nice.

JERRY. She's givin' up a lot for me and I'm gonna make sure her and little Mickey are taken care of real good.

SABRINA. (*To Michael.*) Take him out for a cigarette or something, will you?

MICHAEL. Yeah, uh, Jer, how about a smoke?

JERRY. Groovy man, you carryin'?

MICHAEL. Don't get too excited, they're only Camels. Come on.

SABRINA. (*As soon as THEY leave.*) You can't be serious?

CONNIE. You saw him on an off day.

SABRINA. It's your wedding day, for ...

CONNIE. Pete's sake! I know, I know. He could tell you were making fun of him.

SABRINA. He couldn't tell, trust me.

CONNIE. I love him.

SABRINA. No you don't.

CONNIE. Do to.

SABRINA. Do not.

CONNIE. Do to, do to, do to.

SABRINA. You won't make it through the first year.

CONNIE. Will to.

SABRINA. And what about your kids?

CONNIE. Kid, singular. You're the one going to have kids, plural.

SABRINA. You're running away again, packing your bags and running from responsibility, from people who need you. That's what you're doing, you're running to something that you think will make it all go away instead of facing it here and working it out.

CONNIE. Wait a minute. Is this about me or about you?

SABRINA. You're the one getting married again, you're the one searching for something, not me. I love Michael.

CONNIE. Do you? Didn't you run away too?

SABRINA. From what?

CONNIE. From home, from your mom and the pressures. From everything.

SABRINA. No.

CONNIE. No?

SABRINA. NO!

CONNIE. It's okay, you know. You don't have to keep feeling guilty about it. Your mom will be fine. It's her life and you have one of your own.

SABRINA. What has my mother got to do with this?

CONNIE. Look, I love you. Let's just drop the whole thing, okay?

CONNIE. I'm sorry.

SABRINA. You should be!

CONNIE. You wanted to escape just like I did. Brin, it's okay. My marriage didn't work and I got out, yours is maybe having some problems but you feel guilty about running the first time and you don't wanna do it again. Great. Stay and work it out. I want you and Mikey to make it. But I'm starting over ... I think we should call the guys now.

SABRINA. Sure, call the guys. Turn this whole thing on me. Fine.

CONNIE. What?

SABRINA. At least I didn't run around giving everybody fake names and pretending to be ...

CONNIE. From now on, you're Wanda.

SABRINA. I am.

CONNIE. Fine.

(THEY stand there staring at each other for a moment. BOTH of them wanting to say something, to take it all back but neither of them uttering a sound. MICHAEL and JERRY enter.)

MICHAEL. Well, that was enlightening ... What's with you two?

SABRINA. I just remembered, the baby sitter has to leave early. I don't think we can stay.

CONNIE. Oh, don't give it a thought. (*SHE looks the other way and then back.*) I'll miss you.

MICHAEL. Brina, you're Connie's maid of honor.

SABRINA. Please call me by my given name.

MICHAEL. You really want me to call you Wanda?

CONNIE. Mikey, I'll miss you. Take care, okay? Bye, Bri ... Wanda.

MICHAEL. I hope you both know how really stupid this is. You're both gonna regret it later ...I love ya, Con. Be happy. (*HE kisses her.*) You too, Elvis.

JERRY. Say what?

MICHAEL. Uh, Jerry ... Sorry, Con, I couldn't resist.

JERRY. Yeah ... Hon, I think they're ready for us. Sorry you have to leave. Peace and love, man.

CONNIE. Take care, Mikey. You too ...

(*THEY start to exit as SABRINA and MICHAEL watch.*)

SABRINA. Uh, Jerry, I don't know if this is right or not but "break a leg."

JERRY. At my wedding?

CONNIE. She means in Ontario, at the Pig's Tail ... I'll tell ya later.

JERRY. Oh, okay, thanks. Hey, that's got the making's of a song ... Bend over lemme see ya break a pig's tail ... naw.

(*THEY leave.*
LIGHTS fade and MICHAEL disappears as well, leaving
  SABRINA alone.)

SABRINA. Maybe if I'd've said "shake" instead of "break" ... nooohhh. (*SHE looks around and then moves back to the chair.*) Connie, Connie, Connie. Just look at us. Well, at least you're quiet, that's an all time first!

I never told you this but I used to go to Jimmy B's every Wednesday. I'd hang out in that joint, I'd look for you and listen to "Volare." That was my penance ... Binky had a mad crush on Josie Wynecki and I occupied my time by playing matchmaker. You'd've loved that one! Then all of a sudden on day, there you were sitting right across from me and the two of us pretending not to see one another. Jimmy and Binky both taking turns for over an hour, talking to you and talking to me. Telling us both how silly it was, our not speaking. I wasn't gonna be the one to break the ice. Then Binky played that damned song, your very own favorite and I had to sit through the worst rendition of "That's Amore" known to man! ... God. I'll never know why that was your favorite or what on earth ever made you think you could sing it! We both laughed and I remembered how we'd found that joint when we were just kids. How you loved watching that handsome young waiter, Stanley, with the curly hair. He looked just like Sal Mineo in *Rebel Without a Cause*.

I really wanted to speak. I wanted to hug you, to cry, to ball you out ... but I didn't. I was so stubborn. I just got up and left for my appointment at Dr. Macon's office. Hoping you'd stop me. I didn't even say hello.

(*LIGHTS come up on a doctor's waiting room. SABRINA sits there as CONNIE enters.*)

CONNIE. Not only are you a pushy broad, you're also a stubborn one. So, isn't this a coincidence?

SABRINA. I'm stubborn?

CONNIE. Wanda, Wanda, Wanda ... How the hell are ya?

SABRINA. You can cut the "Wanda" routine. Michael got too used to calling me Brina. I couldn't change it.

CONNIE. Couldn't?

SABRINA. Okay, didn't want to ... So, what are you doing at Dr. Macon's office? Did you follow me?

CONNIE. Such an ego! I'm here for a check-up. I met her when Mattie was born. By the way, how is my little Godchild?

SABRINA. Mattie's fine. She doesn't like to be called "little." She loved all your presents.

CONNIE. We sure wasted a lot of time, huh, kiddo?

SABRINA. Yes.

CONNIE. Mickey's gonna be eight next month and my new one, little Wanda ...

SABRINA. Wanda?!

CONNIE. Just kidding! I wouldn't do that to a kid. Got a rise outta ya, though, didn't I? (*SHE laughs.*)

SABRINA. You'll never change. You may possibly remember, however, I did name Mattie after you.

CONNIE. I know, Brin, but "Wanda"!? ... I did compromise, though. I named her Maria, Louisa, Sophia ... Listen, Brin, I really wanted to see you, to talk ...

(*A female DOCTOR enters.*)

DR. MACON. Hello, Mrs. Roberts. I'll be ready for you in a minute. (*To Connie.*) Mrs. Smiley?

CONNIE. Yes.

DR. MACON. I have your form but you didn't fill in your husband's first name or place of employment.

CONNIE. His name's Timothy. But we're getting divorced. Just bill me.

DR. MACON. You're lucky I had a cancellation. I can't usually see someone within an hour of their phoning me. But I thought as long as you two were coming together. I'll be with you both in a few moments. You know, I may even get out of here early enough to play golf this afternoon. (*SHE exits.*)

SABRINA. Mrs. Smiley? The two of us, coming together?

CONNIE. Yes and almost yes.

SABRINA. I didn't even know you were back in town, you didn't even call me. If I hadn't seen you at Jimmy B's...

CONNIE. Ah ha. I knew you knew I was there. I saw you see me.

SABRINA. See you?! I heard you. Who could possible mistake your singing, "When the moon hitsa your eye like a bigga pizza pie!"

CONNIE. I sing good, huh?

SABRINA. No.

CONNIE. Brina, Brina, you know you love it. Anyway, Binky told me you were coming over here and I needed to see the doc myself, so ... I figured that way we'd have to talk.

SABRINA. (*Hugging her.*) I'm glad Binky volunteered ... told you. And you're right, I am a stubborn ... Hey, let's back up a minute. What about the Mrs. Smiley part?

When did you and Elvis get divorced? Who's the new one or should I even bother to ask?

CONNIE. I tried to call you but you were always out carousin' around. That's when I knew you were at Jimmy B's, lookin' for me. (*SHE settles in for a very long, very animated story. Which is very typically, Connie.*) As for Jerry: He wasn't even going to get drafted. That was a scam … to get attention, make himself look as if he were this dramatic character willing to give up all for freedom and to protest the war. In reality, he had flat feet, wore contact lenses, he was legally blind and his eyes were green not blue, that was from the lenses …

SABRINA. Connie!

CONNIE. You said it wouldn't last a year?

SABRINA. I didn't mean …

CONNIE. Ten months. That's when he really did officially make me his BACK-UP singer.

SABRINA. Hell hath no fury!

CONNIE. So, and this was the absolute final curl on the pig's tail. Oh, God, you won't believe this!

SABRINA. What?

CONNIE. I can't tell you.

SABRINA. Connie, for Pete's sake!

CONNIE. Don't laugh. You have to promise me … you will, you'll laugh.

SABRINA. I won't laugh.

CONNIE. He … no. You will.

SABRINA. I won't, I won't, I won't.

CONNIE. Promise. Cross your heart.

SABRINA. Cross my heart and hope to die.

CONNIE. Stick a needle in your eye?

SABRINA. I hate that part. (*SHE crosses her heart again.*) Stick a needle in my eye. Tell me!

CONNIE. He sang to me.

SABRINA. What? Is that all? I thought he was just like Elvis?

CONNIE. No. That resemblance ended when he opened his mouth. Listen—listen ... what he'd sing was, "Back in the Saddle Again." (*SHE starts to giggle uncontrollably.*)

SABRINA. No! No!

CONNIE. Yes, yes. And it was the times he chose to sing it! (*THEY're both laughing.*) I couldn't keep a straight face or any other part of my body for that matter. Swear to God!

(*THEY both are laughing.*)

TOGETHER. "Back in the Saddle Again"? Whoa ha! Giddy up little heffer ... Ride' em cowboy ... (*THEY're getting hysterical.*) Hoo Rah!

CONNIE. See, I knew you'd laugh.

TOGETHER. Oh, my God!

(*THEY fall on the floor THEY're laughing so hard.. DR. MACON enters.*)

DR. MACON. Is something wrong? ... Oh. You're laughing, children. I didn't know what was going on out here.

CONNIE. (*Trying to stop.*) Oh, sorry. It's just, it's just ... oh, God. (*SHE laughs harder.*)

DR. MACON. Never mind. I'm not sure I want to know. Have fun, just don't sprain anything. Wanda, I'll see you in a few minutes.

(SABRINA shakes her head, unable to talk and the DOCTOR exits.)

CONNIE. So you can see why it didn't work. During the divorce he said I caused him mental anguish. He said I laughed at inappropriate moments!! He said it was detrimental to his career. (*SHE doubles up.*) I told him he should've done that act on stage, maybe he'd of drawn a crowd!

SABRINA. You are as crazy as ever. No wonder I missed the hell outta you. (*Turns CONNIE around checking under her arms and her back.*) Well, you're clean.

CONNIE. Oh, this isn't new.

SABRINA. Well, that explains it.

CONNIE. I should've come home after ... "the fiasco," but that's where I met Timothy. He wasn't running away or anything, he lived there.

SABRINA. But you didn't even tell me.

CONNIE. I didn't wanna admit you were right. I didn't want you to know. I was embarrassed. Besides, the way my luck has been with men, I mean they do come and go ... sometimes they "go" before they "*come.*"

SABRINA. I wondered what ever happened to good ole Roger.

(THEY both giggle.)

CONNIE. So. How's your mom and dad and the kids? I guess everybody's pretty well grown.

SABRINA. Mom died. She had a stroke and then got pneumonia in the hospital.

CONNIE. When?

SABRINA. Right after you left, November 22, '65. I couldn't call you, I didn't know how to reach you. I'd wished you were here.

CONNIE. I'm so sorry. Best friends should never let that happen.

SABRINA. So promise me it won't happen again.

CONNIE. I promise. God, I'm dyin' to see Mr. Peepers. How is the ole man?

SABRINA. Fine. You know Michael. He's the most likable guy we know.

CONNIE. Do I detect a bit of sarcasm?

SABRINA. No. Tell me what you're doing now. About Timothy, about you. Why are you really here?

CONNIE. Timothy's a boring story. Except! Except that he did look exactly like Paul Newman in *Cool Hand Luke*! (*SHE laughs.*) I wanted to come home. I missed you guys, everybody. I have to find out if my dad's come out of the attic or if Mom's still this crazed woman with a baseball bat.

SABRINA. Why are you at the doctor? And don't say it was only to see me.

CONNIE. I ... nothing. A pap smear. The regular female stuff. You?

SABRINA. Same thing.

DR. MACON. (*Comes out.*) Ready for you, ladies. Rooms 3 & 4, please and take ...

CONNIE and SABRINA. ... everything off and put on the paper wind breaker.

DR. MACON. You ladies have done this before!

(SHE smiles and THEY follow her out.
LIGHTS fade and once more come up on SABRINA at the
coffin.)

SABRINA. Paper windbreaker!... I should have known better than trust you with that "I'll call you, we'll get together real soon." I should've known something was wrong. I knew you were more upset than you acted and I didn't think you were pregnant. *That* you would've told me! You always told me everything that had anything to do with sex. (*SHE laughs.*) I even remember the first time it happened and it was you, of course, that beat me to the punch. You couldn't wait to tell me ... right there in front of Hornsby's office.

CONNIE. (*Offstage. Yelling through school hall NOISES.*) Brin! Brina, wait for me ... I have to tell you something!! ... It's real important, don't leave, okay?!

SABRINA. (*Wanders into the scene and yells back.*) 'Kay, I'll wait.

(SHE looks around and then waves off to the distance as
the school BELL rings, doors close and NOISE
subsides. CONNIE comes running in, out of breath.
LIGHTS come up on the principal's waiting area.)

CONNIE. (*Runs in.*) Brin! Brina, you're not gonna believe this ... what're you doin' at Hornsby's office?

SABRINA. I have to leave early, my mom's not feeling good. What's up?

CONNIE. (*Checking to see no one's around.*) Shhhh ... Oh, God, oh God, oh God ... you won't believe this.

SABRINA. What happened?

CONNIE. Only the most important thing, that's all. I've been looking everywhere for you.

SABRINA. Tell me, for Pete's sake!

CONNIE. Move away from the door, I don't want anybody to hear this.

(THEY move to another chair.)

CONNIE. Maybe we should go outside.

SABRINA. Will you stop! Just tell me.

CONNIE. Okay ... we did it.

SABRINA. I'm sure I'm missing something here. Who's "we"?

CONNIE. Oh crimony, Sabrina Anna Louisa, Maria ... Roger's who.

SABRINA. Okay, Roger ... I got the "we" part now what's the ... it! You did "it"?

CONNIE. Shhhh ... you got the "it" part.

SABRINA. When? What was it like? Was there any flashes of lightning? Did you hear bells? Roger? Oh, God, not Roger?

CONNIE. Yes Roger. One question at a time, please.

SABRINA. What was it like?

CONNIE. It hurt.

SABRINA. That's all? It hurt?

CONNIE. No. It really hurt!

SABRINA. It's not supposed to hurt. Is it?

CONNIE. I don't know. I wasn't prepared. It was … big. I didn't know it would be so … big.

SABRINA. I'm sorry.

CONNIE. It took at least a hunnerd tries to even, you know, get it in.

SABRINA. (*Shuddering.*) Where did you …

CONNIE. In Roger's car. Which didn't make it any easier, I might add. He's got four on the floor. I don't recommend it at all if you want the earth to move.

SABRINA. The earth didn't move?

CONNIE. No. But the car did. One time when the gear shift got knocked into low, Roger hadda hurry and put it back into park.

SABRINA. I guess that means it wasn't like Troy Donahue and Sandra Dee in *Summer Place*?

CONNIE. Well, Roger does look like him, in that movie.

SABRINA. So did you or didn't you feel the earth move?

CONNIE. I don't know.

SABRINA. How can you "not know"?

CONNIE. It hurt so much I couldn't tell.

SABRINA. So you're not ever gonna do it again?

CONNIE. Of course I'm gonna do it again, I liked it.

SABRINA. For Pete's sake, Con, did it hurt or did you like it?

CONNIE. Both, I think. I mean I started to like it but it didn't last long.

SABRINA. Whatta ya mean?

CONNIE. By the time I started to like it, it was over. (*SABRINA stares at her.*) Well, Roger says I have to like it a little faster.

(Still staring in disbelief, SABRINA doesn't say anything. Then:)

SABRINA. And how does Roger know?

CONNIE. His sister told him. You know, she's the brunette that ...

SABRINA. ... sits in the back of the show. I know. The one that wears too much Evening in Paris and dates the twins from the rodeo.

CONNIE. Yeah, that's her. Crimony, she should know!

SABRINA. I think she wants to try it out on Michael.

CONNIE. Oh.

SABRINA. So, what about you? What if you got pregnant?

CONNIE. We're going steady now.

SABRINA. Great. Connie, you don't love him. Not like ...

CONNIE. I have to go now.

SABRINA. I'm sorry. Are you still meeting us at the show?

CONNIE. No. I think I'll stay home and listen to records.

SABRINA. "Love Me Tender"?

CONNIE. Sabrina, this was a monumental day. Don't spoil it, okay?

SABRINA. Okay.

CONNIE. Come by after the show, will ya? We could talk.

(LIGHTS fade and SABRINA watches as SHE exits. THEY come up again on the coffin.)

CONNIE. I didn't event go to the show that night. We talked till almost daylight. You played "Volare" and "That's Amore" and we cried all the way through "Love Me Tender" but neither of us mentioned Duggie. I told you that night that Michael and I were getting married and you said maybe you did love Roger. We were scared and excited at the same time. We laughed, we cried, we sang off-key. I didn't ever wanna grow up that night. We wished on the North Star and jumped in the leaves in your back yard. I wanted us to stay that way forever … for time to just come to a dead stop … stand still … but it didn't. If anything it seemed to spin faster after that night. Things began to change. Not a lot at first, but they changed. We didn't have the time to dream or listen to Doris Day sing "Secret Love" or your very own favorite. (*SHE sits down and quietly hums and then begins to smile and sings to Connie's favorite Dean Martin song.*)

END OF ACT I

ACT II

The Funeral attendant enters.

ATTENDANT. Excuse me.

SABRINA. Yes?

ATTENDANT. (*Looking around.*) Oh. I thought I heard…

SABRINA. I was just talking to my friend. (*HE looks around and SABRINA points to the coffin.*) My friend.

ATTENDANT. Oh! Well, I just thought I should mention that we close in half an hour. Last pot of coffee's … I forgot. Caffeine makes you crazy. (*HE smiles.*)

SABRINA. Right.

ATTENDANT. Doesn't she have any family?

SABRINA. Yes, she has family. I'm family and she has kids and husbands, and maybe even a father in an attic somewhere.

ATTENDANT. Ah, ha … well …

SABRINA. I'd like to visit a while longer.

ATTENDANT. Of course. (*HE leaves, looking over his shoulder as HE does.*)

SABRINA. I don't know how you do it, kiddo. He looks just like Al Pacino in *The Godfather*!! Of course, he thinks I'm completely whacko.

I just had the funniest thought! You, running bare-assed through Dr. Macon's office … paper windbreaker flapping! … I should've know something was wrong that day. You hated doctors, you never went voluntarily, not ever. Why

49

in the Sam hell I didn't ask you what was wrong ... Who knows?... So you go through a damned hysterectomy all by yourself, the same time you're going through the second ... *no, third,* divorce and don't say a word, you actually avoid me, for Pete's sake! ... Just so you won't "burden" me or Michael with "your" problems. No wonder you tried to kill yourself!

(LIGHTS come up and CONNIE is in a visiting room of hospital in a gown.)

CONNIE. I did not try to kill myself!! What? Are you nuts?!
SABRINA. Oh, no?
CONNIE. No. It was a stupid accident.
SABRINA. I'll go along with the "stupid" part.
CONNIE. I didn't wanna worry you. Besides, this was nothing more than a very large headache, honest.
SABRINA. Ah ha.
CONNIE. Seriously. Timothy, the last one, had filed for divorce ... I wouldn't give up my country and become a Canadian. Sure, I was angry about some of the things my country was doing but I wasn't about to give it up. That's when the kids and I came back, alone. My sister took Mickey and Maria "just to help me out till I got settled" and then refused to give them back. I quote, "Your life style, Madeline, is not conducive to raising children." At the time, I was working with the underground Times, the movement. My salary was food and a shared loft, so she was right, right?
SABRINA. Wrong!

CONNIE. Anyway, I find out, the day I saw you at Dr. Macon's office, that I need a hysterectomy. Okay, I can accept this and get through it, I'm a tough broad ... So, I do. Then, I get out and really find a *job*, a real *job*. so I can get my kids back and have a "conducive" life style, whatever that means ... An' I'm on my way to this tremendously exciting opportunity to become a file clerk for the government, entry level GS 1/2, which, incidentally, gives me this uncontrollable urge to laugh ...

SABRINA. Okay.

CONNIE. Now, to top it all off, the race riots in Watts are getting worse and even on this end of the map me and my car pool, Carol, a teenager, and Ruby, this elderly black lady, are ourselves in grave danger. Yours truly ignoring that fact as usual. Carol, our teeny bopper, doesn't read the newspaper so she's completely oblivious and totally unconcerned ... but Ruby, who realizes far better than me the danger, amazingly still has this incredible sense of humor ... I gotta tell ya this, you'll love it.

SABRINA. Ah, ha.

CONNIE. Carol, bless her heart, is driving ... Ruby's in the middle and I'm riding shotgun ... an appropriate title for my position during that particular ride. Ruby, reading the morning headlines, suddenly comes up with this great analogy. She blurts out that she feels like a piece of well-done beef between two slices of white bread about to be eaten! Then adds, "I'm sure glad we ain't in Los Angeles." (*SHE laughs nervously, obviously upset.*) Well, we roared. Then someone on the street screams, "Nigger lovers," and throws a rock, hitting my window. It doesn't hurt us, the window's rolled up, but it wasn't funny anymore. (*Pause.*)

I leave work that day and Carol, poor scared child, has disappeared, whoosh, no ride. Ruby's son picks her up and offers to drive me home as well. He drops Ruby off first, 'cause I'm on the way to his apartment, and when he gets to my street, I'm feeling suddenly terrified, sick and ashamed of myself. I tell him I live on a dead-end street, that he can drop me off on the corner. (*SHE is starting to cry now, in spite of herself.*) JESUS, I TELL HIM THIS! ... Oh, he knows I'm lying, of course, that I'm really afraid to be seen with him. (*SHE stops, takes a deep breath and laughs nervously.*) But ... being the gentleman he is, he stops and drops me at the corner ... It was actually just the proverbial, final straw atop what was becoming a major migraine. It was too much ... I get out and practically run inside. Then I proceed to bawl my head off and take a few aspirin ... Problem was, I took more than the allotted eight in any given twenty-four hour period!!

(*SHE stops. SABRINA sits staring at her. Silence.*)

SABRINA. Oh, brother! (*SHE suddenly grabs her and hugs her.*)
CONNIE. At least you didn't say "for Pete's sake!" (*SHE starts to laugh.*)
SABRINA. It isn't funny, Con. You could have really hurt yourself. I don't wanna lose you.
CONNIE. It was dumb. Anybody with any smarts would've known that all I'd end up with is a really bad stomach ache and a trip to ... (*SHE falls back on the couch.*) Da psychiatrist's couch!
SABRINA. Well. You need your head examined.
CONNIE. Agreed.

SABRINA. Dammit, you don't kill yourself, you call me and we go have Blue Nun, sing "That's Amore" and solve the world's problems together, remember?

CONNIE. I didn't wanna kill myself. I mean reeaallly, Brin, Bayer Aspirin?! Come on. So, you're right, we'll go have Blue Nun, you, me and Mikey. (*SABRINA doesn't answer.*) Something wrong?

SABRINA. No.

CONNIE. Oh, now who's not talking?

SABRINA. You never burden me so I see no reason to burden you.

CONNIE. Touché. So enough of this silliness. What's wrong? You and Michael having problems?

SABRINA. We're separated.

CONNIE. I leave you two alone for a few years and look what happens.

SABRINA. Remember when you married Elvis and you told me I was feeling guilty about leaving home, running away from the responsibility of raising my brother and sister and taking care of my mom and that I was only staying with Michael 'cause I was afraid I'd just be running away again and I couldn't face that?

CONNIE. I said all that?

SABRINA. Not exactly in those words but that's what I was really feeling.

CONNIE. Oh.

SABRINA. So. I took your advice and left.

CONNIE. (*Feigning a faint.*) Herr doctor, it's my friend you should examine, she's the crazy one. She's taking *my* advice!

SABRINA. I happen to think you were right.

CONNIE. For Pete's sake. You never thought I was right about anything. Except maybe that James Reddig was an asshole and that Mr. Pedigre did not have a drop! You guys have been together forever. You have two weird but very cute kids.

SABRINA. I just had to leave. Things were closing in on me.

CONNIE. We're goin' to hell in a handbasket, as my mother used to say.

SABRINA. I know.

CONNIE. Okay. We're gonna start over. We'll do a time warp. I'll get my act together and get the kids.

SABRINA. I already got them ...

(CONNIE is shocked and surprised.)

SABRINA. It wasn't so tough. I just threatened your sister with telling her husband about the night she and James Reddig ... (*SHE whispers in Connie's ear.*)

CONNIE. ALL RIGHT!

SABRINA. (*Nods.*) So the kids are all together, at my house.

CONNIE. (*Hugs her.*) You're a genius.

SABRINA. So, you're okay?

CONNIE. I'm alive, my stomach's not but I am. I have a best friend who looks like SABRINA and I AM SINGLE AGAIN! What more could a girl ask? (*SHE stops as DR. HAUSLER enters.*) Except for maybe ...

DR. HAUSLER. Vell, vell. How are ve doink this morgning?

CONNIE. Great! Uh, Doc, this is my best friend, Sabrina Roberts.

SABRINA. (*To Connie.*) How do you do it? (*To the doctor.*) Good morg ... uh, morning.

CONNIE. Is it time for our session, Doc?

SABRINA. I can see the writing on the wall.

DR. HAUSLER. Such a villing patient. No, I come to brink you gut news. You are going home tomorrow, no?

CONNIE. I am?

DR. HAUSLER. Yes. You are doink fine. We can have our little sessions at my office, no?

CONNIE. Can't think of a single reason.

SABRINA. I didn't think so.

DR. HAUSLER. (*To Sabrina.*) You vill keep an eye on our little patient, eh? See she does not take anymore aspirin bottles, no?

SABRINA. No. I mean, yes. I think.

DR. HAUSLER. Gut! Ve vouldn't vant to lose her, vould ve? Now, you finish da visit and come see me ven Sabrina leaves. Nice to meet you. (*HE kisses her hand and hugs CONNIE then exits.*)

SABRINA. What a hunk! He looks just like ...

CONNIE. Clark Gable in *Gone With The Wind*!

SABRINA. Yes, he does.

CONNIE. He certainly curls my pajama bottoms.

SABRINA. Connie, don't scare me like that again, will ya?

CONNIE. Promise.

SABRINA. How did everything go with the surgery, the hysterectomy. Are you all right?

CONNIE. Great. I can't get pregnant and I don't have to take the pill.

SABRINA. It doesn't affect your ...

CONNIE. My sex life? Will Superman always save Lois Lane? Is Scarlett O'Hara nuts for wanting Ashley over Rhett Butler? My sex life? Are you kidding?

SABRINA. I heard it can make you depressed, maybe lose your sex drive.

CONNIE. Me, lose my sex drive?! Are you crazy? You're right about one thing, though, *that* would tend to make a girl think about suicide.

SABRINA. Con!

CONNIE. Just kidding … Okay. I had a small problem at first, but Doc's helping me work all that out.

SABRINA. Dr. Hausler?!

CONNIE. (*Laughing.*) Wishful thinking, Brin. No. I talk to him and take this little yellow pill every day, Premarin. He and Dr. Macon both assured me I won't grow a mustache, start spitting out of car windows or scratching my crotch in public.

SABRINA. I'm so relieved.

CONNIE. I did have a minor scare, though. I meet this woman in the hospital, the morning of my surgery, right after Dr. Macon tells me everything has to go, okay?

SABRINA. Oh, no.

CONNIE. So this woman, in the hallway right outside the operating room, no less, starts talking to me. Here we are lined up like an assembly and, next to me, I get Weirdo of the Year!

SABRINA. Of course.

CONNIE. So I'm a little buzzed from the drruuggs … but I hear her saying she's already had her hysto a few years back and she's praying for me. She tells me I'll be fine except for … "Except for what?" I ask her. "Nothing," she tells me. Oh, no, you don't do that to me, buzzed or awake! "Except for what?!" I say again. I tell her, "Listen, I really like sex," I know this sounds funny, right, but I wanna know, if that's what she's talkin' about. (*Pause.*) "Well," she says, "we'll talk after the operation." Oh, no! I wanna know right that second. I wanna know what the hell this broad's talkin' about. Nobody's wheeling me in this room till I know ... I've practically got her by the jugular at this point.

(SHE laughs as SABRINA sits amazed.)

CONNIE. "Well," she tells me, "you can forget about sex. Just forget about it and go on with your life." (*SHE laughs.*) You don't just say, "forget about sex," not to me, right? So I gotta pursue this ridiculous conversation.
SABRINA. Maybe she just ...
CONNIE. Wait, wait. You gotta hear this. So I tell her, "Listen, miss, I really like sex, I mean reeaally like it. I can't just forget about it." Now she looks me right square in the eye and asks me, "Do you know much about farms?" "What?! Farms?!" I ask her. Now I'm thinking this broad is looney toons, right? What the hell does farming have to do with a hysto? And she adds, quite nonchalantly, "Honey, why the hell do you think they castrate pigs?"
SABRINA. My God.
CONNIE. It gave me something to think about when they told me to count backwards from a hundred, I can tell you that! I mean I'm picturing this oinker runnin' around with my face, turning down all the best lookin' pigs in the pigpen, eating my way across the mud pile!
SABRINA. You're too damn skinny to be an oinker but if you were a little piglet, all of the best looking male

piggies'd be working over time to get your attention. Hell, if I know you, you'd end up with the one that looked just like Porky Pig in that cartoon!!

(THEY both hug and laugh as the LIGHTS fade and CONNIE disappears.
LIGHTS come up as SABRINA sits quietly at the coffin.)

SABRINA. Well ain't this a bitch!?
ATTENDANT. (*Enters.*) Oh, you're alone.
SABRINA. Knowing my friend, she didn't tell anyone she'd be here.
ATTENDANT. Most of our clients have a difficult time doing that. (*SHE doesn't answer.*) I thought I saw the young man come in here.
SABRINA. Young man?
ATTENDANT. I think he's the same gentleman who paid her expenses.
SABRINA. That must have been who called me. Robert DeNiro in *Falling in Love*!
ATTENDANT. Excuse me?
SABRINA. Not the real one but I'll bet he looked just like him in that movie.
ATTENDANT. I don't understand.
SABRINA. Not many people did.
ATTENDANT. Yes. Well, I just thought ... I must have been wrong. We're getting ready to close up shop.
SABRINA. Shhhh. Don't mention that word, "shop." Connie has been known to die for that word ... You know, "Wait'll you see what I bought, it's to die for!"?
ATTENDANT. (*Backs away.*) Sorry. (*HE leaves.*)

SABRINA. (*Laughing*.) Okay, my perpetual teenage friend, was it Robert DeNiro or did you finally find your James Dean in *East of Eden*? You know, I actually envied you. You believed someday you'd really find him and so did I. (*SHE strokes the coffin.*) I was jealous. You had it all. Beauty, brains, personality. But money never was very important to you. Life, living it, loving it, that made you happy. I remember your formula. Your six "L's" for success plan. Love, laugh, look 'em square in the eye, listen to what they say, lust after life and leave lots of good memories behind ... You certainly did that. (*Pause*.) You loved men, lots of them! And they sure as hell felt the same way about you. (*SHE laughs and pats the coffin.*) I called Maria and Mickey. They're flying in tonight. They were planning a surprise party for your 50th birthday. I can't remember you ever getting past eighteen. Oh, and Michael, he and I are back together. That ought to make you feel smug. You always told me we would do that. I haven't told him yet, about you. He was working and I wanted to see you by myself first. Just you and me, kiddo...

Carrie's married and lives in Denver now. D'I tell you that? Mattie's little boys are growing like weeds. They live with us, I keep forgetting, did you know that? There was so much of my life I'd forgotten, isn't that funny and now it's all coming back. So many memories and here I am, getting them all back from you. You taking care of me, just like old times. No matter what I did, no matter how awful I was ... you never stopped caring, being my best friend.

(LIGHTS come up on a funeral setting but it's not the same funeral. CONNIE enters as SABRINA sits by the coffin.)

CONNIE. Brina, I'm so sorry. Oh, God, that's not enough, I'm, I'm … I don't know what to say.

SABRINA. I'm glad you're here. How's New York? You look great.

CONNIE. I don't feel so great.

SABRINA. I saw you in the Bayer Aspirin commercial … How do you stay so slim? Michael's in by the coffin. He'll be so glad to see you. Can I get you some coffee?

(CARRIE enters.)

CARRIE. I'll get it, Mom. Hello Aunt Connie. *(SHE hugs her.)*

CONNIE. My, God, you've gotten so grown up. Such a knock out!

SABRINA. She is. Have you seen Mattie yet? She wanted to be an actress like you. Did you know that?

CONNIE. I actually wanted to be a rock 'n roll star, remember?

SABRINA. Binky always liked your singing. But then, Binky was tone deaf.

(THEY laugh and then suddenly start to cry as THEY hug each other.)

SABRINA. Oh, Con, I had no idea there was anything even wrong. I didn't know she was doing anything with drugs.

CONNIE. I know. It's all right.

CARRIE. Are you still living in New York, Aunt Connie?

CONNIE. No. I'm back for good. I called your mom when I got back.

SABRINA. She did. But you know your Aunt Connie, every time we were supposed to get together something came up. (*SHE stops.*) No, that's not completely true. I was too busy with the business, with making money and trying to be "successful" and I cancelled more than she did. I guess I misplaced the "L" plan somewhere along the line.

CONNIE. You had a better plan. You're really doing well ... I guess that means lust is not the answer!

(*SABRINA doesn't answer, SHE just sits drinking coffee.*)

CARRIE. Excuse me, Aunt Connie, could you turn toward me a minute and raise your right arm?

(*CONNIE does and CARRIE removes a tag from under her arm.*)

CONNIE. What ... I could've sworn I took that thing off.

CARRIE. There, I got it. You should install one of those alarms that goes off when you walk out your front door. You know, the kind they have in department stores.

SABRINA. (*Laughs.*) You did that on purpose, didn't you? (*CONNIE shrugs.*) I'm glad you're here.

(*CARRIE gets the coffee and CONNIE sits down.*)

CONNIE. Me, too.

SABRINA. Carrie, did I ever tell you about the time your dad and Connie and I took a ride in Forest Park?

CARRIE. I don't think so.

CONNIE. Brina, no.

SABRINA. Well, it seems your Aunt Connie's date cancelled on her when he found out she was only sixteen.

CONNIE. He actually got sick or something ...

SABRINA. She had told him she was twenty-one. He was at least twenty-five and very handsome. He looked a little like ...

CONNIE. Like Errol Flynn, but you wouldn't remember him, Car.

SABRINA. So, he didn't wanna rob the cradle ...

CONNIE. Well, I was outta the cradle. But your mom's right, he called me and told me his grandmother died and he had to go to the funeral.

SABRINA. Of course his grandparents were both alive and well and living in Clayton.

CONNIE. Sad but true.

CARRIE. Oh, how mean.

SABRINA. No, Connie thought the whole thing was funny. But Michael found out and he thought she was upset so he didn't wanna leave her home alone.

CONNIE. I was once again the third wheel to your mom and dad's romantic afternoon in the park.

SABRINA. Well. Michael decided he wants to ... you know, do a little necking.

CONNIE. Nothing could stand in the way of romance, not even me.

SABRINA. So your dad wants to jump in the back to neck ...

CARRIE. Dad?! I didn't think he liked that stuff.

SABRINA. Well, not now, but he did then.

CONNIE. Oh yes, he certainly did then!

SABRINA. So he doesn't exactly know what to do with Connie ... so he pulls over and asks her if she'd like to drive.

CONNIE. Ah, ha, he asked me.

SABRINA. Well, he thought you knew how.

CARRIE. You didn't know how?

CONNIE. I had a couple of lessons, in the parking lot.

SABRINA. She didn't know how! Anyway, he pulls over behind the zoo, near the bird cage. That was before they put up all the fences.

CONNIE. That was the reason they put up all those fences.

CARRIE. Oh, no.

SABRINA. It was even worse than that. So, Connie gets behind the wheel, she's being very adult, you know ...

MICHAEL. (*Enters and takes over.*) And your mom and I jump in the back.

CONNIE. Don't ask what they were doing, these are your parents we're talking about.

MICHAEL. All of a sudden, just when your mom and I are ... getting comfortable, there's this huge surge and we hit this bump. We go flying in the air ...

SABRINA. Hit our heads on the roof of the car and find out Connie's jumped the curb!

MICHAEL. And there's this big crash and water is squirting everywhere ... it's not bad enough we've managed to jump the curb, travel forty feet across the walkway and the grass, break through the wire mesh fence that keeps the birds inside, but there's also a loud siren heading our way and getting louder by the minute.

CONNIE. It wasn't really that bad.

MICHAEL. That's when she tells me she doesn't have a license!

CONNIE. How many years did you know me, Michael Roberts? You didn't know I didn't have a license?

SABRINA. Your dad's doing a circus act trying to get over the seat ...

CONNIE. While adjusting a few minor clothing details...

MICHAEL. Your mom and Connie are laughing their heads off ...

SABRINA. Well there was this big bird sitting on the steering wheel and water is squirting right through the floor board.

CONNIE. Just as Michael gets his right leg over the seat there's this policeman tapping on the windshield.

SABRINA. I never laughed so hard!

MICHAEL. I wasn't laughing.

CONNIE. No. But you did laugh later, much later.

SABRINA. It's a good thing you didn't make it over the seat and Connie was still behind the wheel.

CONNIE. Yeah. I told the cop that it was an accident, that I wasn't driving, I was just trying to turn on the radio while they made out.

MICHAEL. She had to add THAT part.

CONNIE. He loved THAT part.

MICHAEL. He took us all into the station.

CONNIE. My dad even had to come out of the attic for that one. I was grounded for the rest of my life!

MICHAEL. My insurance would only pay for the bird cage!

CONNIE and SABRINA. We had to fix Mikey's car out of our tips at Steak 'n Shake and his money from ushering at the Ivanhoe show.

(*THEY all three laugh for a minute and then MICHAEL hugs Connie.*)

CONNIE. You look so young, Michael. You never age.

MICHAEL. I aged a lot this week.

CONNIE. I'm so sorry.

MICHAEL. I didn't know. I thought she was fine. No, no we didn't think she was fine but we didn't know it was that bad. She went back to college, did Brina tell you?

SABRINA. Michael, sit down. I'll go back to the coffin for awhile.

CARRIE. I'll go. You two stay here a few more minutes. (*SHE leaves.*)

MICHAEL. She's a good girl. Like her sister. You know, Mattie was really trying to get her life back together after the divorce. She and the baby came back home. I didn't know it was so hard on her.

SABRINA. She couldn't do the divorce thing as easily as you could, Connie.

MICHAEL. (*Looks at her, surprised, and then goes on.*) Divorce is never easy. (*SABRINA looks away.*) But she was trying. Studying hard. Making new friends.

SABRINA. Getting into drugs.

CONNIE. Are they absolutely sure it was drugs?

SABRINA. They did an autopsy, for chrissake. They did that to my little girl.

MICHAEL. They said it was massive heart failure from the cocaine.

CONNIE. I think I ...

SABRINA. (*Cutting in.*) She was so tired. I should've seen it.

MICHAEL. No, you couldn't of seen it, you were working, trying to keep everything going ... I should have helped more. I should've been there more even though you and I ...

SABRINA. We were divorced, Michael. You couldn't of done anymore than you did. I didn't expect you to. She was grown. She wanted to be like me, tough. She said if I could work and go to school, so could she. I encouraged her to be strong.

CONNIE. It's the drugs I don't understand. It's so damned hard being a young adult. I mean we smoked a little pot, we ...

SABRINA. You ... you smoked a little pot.

CONNIE. I mean, we didn't do anything heavy.

SABRINA. Who knows what you did. I used to try and figure you out. I couldn't.

CONNIE. Brina.

MICHAEL. Nobody did anything like that. Not any of us. And when they told me about Mattie, I couldn't believe it. I thought they were full of shit, that they had her mixed up with some other ...

SABRINA. Corpse?

CONNIE. Brina, are you okay?

SABRINA. Where the fuck did it come from, cocaine!?

CONNIE. I don't know. We didn't have this kind of problem with it when we were young. The only serious problem we had was heroin and I only remember that because of that movie with Frank Sinatra, *The Man with the Golden Arm*, remember? I mean nobody "did it."

SABRINA. You and your goddamned movies! Isn't anything ever real to you?

MICHAEL. She didn't mean it that way. What's wrong with you?

SABRINA. You always stick up for her. (*SHE stops.*) Why does anybody take drugs? (*Back to Connie.*) Why did you? Why did my little girl? Why did she wanna be like you? I know it was hard on them when you and I split up, Michael. I know the girls were mad at me. It was a big responsibility for them, taking care of themselves and the house and school while I worked. It wasn't your fault, Michael, you gave us everything you could. I know when Mattie ran away …

MICHAEL. Ran away?

SABRINA. Left home and got married. I know she was angry, that she wanted to be free. I made a lot of mistakes. I was only thinking of myself, wanting to be a "success," whatever that is. If I hadn't listened to other people and if I hadn't wanted all those things, she'd be here today. She wouldn't have started taking that crap or sniffing it or whatever the hell it is you do with it! She'd be sitting here now, talking to us and laughing instead of lying in there with her goddamned arms folded across her chest!!

CONNIE. (*Grabs her and hugs her.*) Don't say that. Don't think it. You're the best mother I've ever known. It was not your fault.

SABRINA. I should've seen it.

CONNIE. I didn't tell you this but Mickey had a problem with cocaine. I was really scared. He had the worst time trying to get away from it and ended up at a hospital. I didn't understand it either.

SABRINA. Oh, no? I can. I can understand it with Mickey.

MICHAEL. Brina, for God's sake.

SABRINA. Why wouldn't your kids have problems? Why wouldn't they be confused? Why wouldn't they become drug addicts?

(CONNIE backs away, not able to say anything.)

SABRINA. You run away from everything, you always have. You think it's good to run away from order and commitment ... from any kind of conformity. Why shouldn't they? Mickey's just like you. Why, why if he had a problem, why is he still alive and Mattie dead? How is that fair? Why did I ever, ever jinx Mattie with your name?! (*SHE stops suddenly. Realizing what she's just said, SHE starts toward her but suddenly can't move.*) Oh, my God. I didn't mean ...

(CONNIE doesn't move, MICHAEL doesn't move. It's as if THEY are all frozen. The LIGHTS begin to change to reds and then to an eerie surreal effect. MICHAEL and CONNIE disappear.)

SABRINA. I didn't mean it, Con. I was so sorry from the minute it came out. I don't even know why it happened or how you ever forgave me. When you walked away, I wanted to run after to you, to grab you and pull you back, to scream, "forgive me" ... but suddenly I couldn't move. I couldn't open my mouth. The world was just spinning around me. I was this distant observer. My mind seemed to roll back into some godforsaken asylum. Removed from reality, farther and farther away until I just seemed to disappear altogether. I was alone but not alone ... Safe but not safe. Listening but not hearing the screams. My screams. I was in a place where no one could reach me and all I wanted to do was hide, forget, disappear. (*SHE sits down, drained from the experience.*) My God! I remembered. Connie, I remembered the breakdown ... the funeral ... us. How could you forgive me? ... How? ... You never, ever mentioned it again. (*SHE leans her head against the coffin.*)

(*LIGHTS fade and we come up on a hospital waiting room. The same one Connie had been in. SABRINA sits staring into space. Oblivious to everything around her.*)

MICHAEL. (*Entering with the DOCTOR.*) You really think shock treatments will help? That she needs them ... Will they take away her pain?

DR. HAUSLER. Take away the memory of the pain. She may loose some other memory as vell ... ve can't tell. Healing of the mind is very complex thing, no? Ve'll know more after the treatments.

MICHAEL. I hope you're right.

CONNIE. (*Entering in a tither.*) Michael, I'm so glad you're here. I keep trying to see Brina. They keep saying "family members only." Don't they know I'm family?

DR. HAUSLER. Mrs. Smiley, so nice to see you.

MICHAEL. Con, I'm sorry. I didn't think, the doctors didn't think ...

CONNIE. Obviously. If you had, I'd have seen her by now ... oh, Doc, it's not Smiley, it's Bartoli ... but probably not for too much longer. Where's ... (*SHE sees her.*) ... Brin!

(*SABRINA just stares into space but there's a glimmer of recognition, of response.*)

DR. HAUSLER. I think you're seeing Mrs. Roberts is gut.

CONNIE. (*Approaches Sabrina without waiting.*) Hi ya, kiddo. How the hell are ya? So, you'd stop at nothing to get an inside shot at Dr. Hausler, huh? Okay. But, darlin' there are easier ways to meet men.

SABRINA. (*Struggling to get the words out.*) There are?

MICHAEL. (*Shocked.*) Brina? Honey, you said ... you spoke ... Connie, she talked.

CONNIE. Well goddam, Michael, I believe she learned that trick somewhere in the neighborhood of forty-five years ago. Give her mother, not me, credit for that skill ... So, when the hell ya gettin' outta here, kid? I am back and we're gonna start raisin' a little hell. I have more guys lined up that wanna meet you.

SABRINA. Do any of them wear little round glasses and have three or maybe four white hairs sticking out of the top of their heads?

CONNIE. God! I hope not. But then, I have been known to attract a few weirdos in my day.

DR. HAUSLER. Are you feeling all right, Wanda?

SABRINA. My friends call me Sabrina.

DR. HAUSLER. All right. (*HE squeezes her hand.*) I'll talk with you after your friend leaves. Not too long now. (*HE exits.*)

CONNIE. Ah, ha. Und he never did any of zee erotic hand holding ven I vas his patient.

SABRINA. Eat your heart out ... He looks just like ... like ... who was it he looked like?

CONNIE. Clark ... Uh, I never gave him one, you do it.

SABRINA. Like ... Charles Boyer?

CONNIE. Charles Boyer, yeah, that's a good one.

SABRINA. In what movie? I can't remember a movie.

CONNIE. So what? Neither can I.

MICHAEL. Honey, I've been so worried. I love you, Brin.

CONNIE. Sure. You let her get away from you once and now that she's a gorgeous single lady with numerous admirers lined up to meet her, the Peep's worried!

SABRINA. Michael, I'm so sorry about all this, about putting you through ...

MICHAEL. You didn't put me through anything. There's nothing to be sorry about.

SABRINA. I feel sick, like something awful ...

CONNIE. You're okay now.

SABRINA. The funeral. Oh, God, Mattie's funeral.

MICHAEL. It's over. She's buried next to your mother like you wanted. I'm staying at the house with Carrie and there's only one thing we want you to do and that's get well.

CONNIE. She's on her way.

SABRINA. The boys. They're with you? (*MICHAEL nods.*) Con, I said something ...

CONNIE. You did?

MICHAEL. (*Starting to cry.*) Brin, I do love you.

CONNIE. Oh, for Pete's sake, Mikey. Is this gonna get mushy?

SABRINA. I love you too. Both of you. Michael, do you mind if Connie and I talk a few minutes?

MICHAEL. Sure. I'll get some coffee.

SABRINA. It's just, I have something …

MICHAEL. I know. I'll be in the cafeteria. Come down and have coffee when you're through, Con. Brina, you'll get some rest?

SABRINA. Rest? That's all I've done since …

MICHAEL. (*Hugs her and then Connie.*) It's okay … Did I tell you how good it is to see you, Con?

CONNIE. No, but better late than never. Go.

(HE smiles and exits.)

CONNIE. I take it the thirty-year-old love affair is back in bloom?

SABRINA. I hope so. Connie, I didn't think I'd ever see you again. Something happened, something … I said something …

CONNIE. What's new? You're always saying something. I always thought you were jealous of this exciting and glamorous life I lead.

SABRINA. I was.

CONNIE. Well so was I, of you.

SABRINA. No. I never had your courage. I always played it safe.

CONNIE. No, Brin. It was important. I mean you're the one who stayed married and had a home and two weird but very cute ... (*SHE stops suddenly.*)

SABRINA. It's okay ... You're back now for good? No more New York City and career? Who'd you get involved with this time?!

CONNIE. It's not important.

SABRINA. Ah ha.

SABRINA. So, hey. Does this mean our days of single dating bliss are over? I don't think you ever even got a jump start.

SABRINA. I wasn't cut out for it. It doesn't work for me like it does you.

CONNIE. Like it does me?!!!

SABRINA. You know what I mean. (*SHE struggles for a minute to get the words together.*) I had a few brain cells bite the dust. Some due to being plugged into the hospital light socket but some seemed to have burned out on their own here and there. I do, however, remember what it was like trying to date after Michael and I split up.

CONNIE. And you thought I was having fun all those years.

SABRINA. Lemme put it this way. Concerning the mystical world of dating, there are several horror stories that I will never forget.

CONNIE. Oh?

SABRINA. Take my word for it. Let's say, for instance, that there were one hundred guys in one room, and ninety-five of the hundred were nice guys.

CONNIE. Ah, ha.

SABRINA. And the other five were ... fuckheads?!

CONNIE. I get the picture.

SABRINA. Well, I'd pick one of the fuckheads.
CONNIE. Don't feel bad. I'd marry the other four!!

(THEY both laugh.)

SABRINA. I'm gonna cool it for awhile, have Michael come home. He belongs there. He loves Mattie's boys and I'm gonna need a lot of help. I'm raising another family all over again.
CONNIE. That's what you do best.
SABRINA. What if I can't do a better job? What if …
CONNIE. You didn't do anything wrong the first time. You always do this. Panic.
SABRINA. I do?
CONNIE. Yes. Since the beginning. Like the time we all went to Meremac Caverns. You and me and Roger and Michael.
SABRINA. I don't remember that …
CONNIE. Well. Roger, he was such an asshole, and he was being his typical obnoxious self that day. He caused us to get separated from the guide and you panicked. You were sooo dramatic.
SABRINA. I was?
CONNIE. You said we'd be lost down there forever. That we'd probably starve and be found as remains. You saw this roped-off place where they had petrified wood and old mule bones from some miners who'd camped there a hundred years before and you said, "Bones around a campfire, that's all we'll be." *(SHE laughs.)*
SABRINA. Did we ever get out?

(THEY both laugh.)

CONNIE. Will Superman always save Lois Lane?

SABRINA. Was Scarlett O'Hara an idiot for wanting Ashley over Rhett Butler?

CONNIE. Have I been married four times?

SABRINA. Is the Pope ... wait a minute. Four?

CONNIE. Bartoli. Last name's Bartoli now.

SABRINA. When? Did I know?

CONNIE. I was lonely while you were gone. I went to Jimmy B's one night and this great-looking guy comes in, sits down next to me and he looks just like Marcello Mastrianni.

SABRINA. In what movie?

CONNIE. I don't know. I can't think of one. Anyway, he orders us both a glass of Blue Nunn and proceeds to play my favorite song on the jukebox. Do you remember my favorite song?

SABRINA. *That* I wish I could forget.

CONNIE. So, we start talking and the next thing you know ...

(LIGHTS fade and CONNIE disappears. A YOUNG MAN enters. HE's wearing an Army uniform and HE looks a lot like Duggie.)

DOUGLAS. Excuse me.

SABRINA. (*Turning, SHE is shocked.*) Duggie?!

DOUGLAS. No, mam. Douglas. Douglas Tanner. I was Connie's friend ... I was more than a friend. I was in love with her.

(SABRINA sits down.)

DOUGLAS. Sorry if I scared you.

SABRINA. No, you didn't scare me, exactly. I thought ... never mind. Are you the young man who phoned me?

DOUGLAS. Yes, mam. She talked about you all the time, said you were her best friend. She said I should call you ... right before, right before ... (*HE starts to break down and sits.*) I didn't know who else to call. She never introduced me to her kids. She was embarrassed, I think, of being with me. She said I was too young for her.

SABRINA. Connie said that?

DOUGLAS. Yes, mam. She wasn't though, she was everything I wanted, more than I ever hoped I'd find.

SABRINA. You said you were in love with her?

DOUGLAS. I know she didn't believe me but I was. (*HE stops and goes to the coffin.*) She was the sunshine every morning.

SABRINA. My God. You really did come back.

DOUGLAS. Mam? ...

(*SABRINA just shakes her head.*)

DOUGLAS. I wouldn't have left without telling you hello, and introducing myself. I'd like to keep in touch, write ... (*HE starts to cry.*) It was my fault.

SABRINA. What?

DOUGLAS. It was, I know it was.

SABRINA. You're in the Army?

DOUGLAS. Reserves, I just got called up ... it's been so fast, I didn't even tell 'er yet. I'm goin' to the Gulf.

SABRINA. She didn't know?

DOUGLAS. No, mam. I was gonna tell her tomorrow before I had to report.

SABRINA. I'm glad.

DOUGLAS. Yes, mam.

SABRINA. Sabrina, please. I hate being called mam almost as much as I did Wanda.

DOUGLAS. I still can't believe this happened. I hope you don't mind my payin' for the funeral. I wanted to do something.

SABRINA. Of course not. She told me about you. She did love you, you know.

DOUGLAS. I really do feel like it was my fault ...

(SABRINA starts to interrupt again but HE stops her.)

DOUGLAS. It was ... we were ... we ... (*HE stops and moves away, uncomfortable.*) I was gonna ask her to marry me. She probably woulda turned me down. She always laughed when I tried to talk about it, she laughed. Not mean, she just said that was something she did a lot but this time it wasn't right. She didn't wanna hurt me.

SABRINA. (*Sensing his discomfort.*) She cared more than you know.

DOUGLAS. She was so different.

SABRINA. That she was.

DOUGLAS. This is ... hard for me to say ... I mean ... I might be talkin' outta turn here, but she said you knew her better than anybody. I just have to say this ... tell somebody ...

SABRINA. Yes?

DOUGLAS. I wanted to make love to her. I begged her to make love to me. I really wanted to make love to her more than anybody I'd ever known.

SABRINA. So you think maybe you're a sex maniac?

DOUGLAS. No, mam, it wasn't ...

SABRINA. Just kidding.

DOUGLAS. She loved me, too, I could tell. No matter what she said, she loved me ... I just wanted her so much, wanted to hold 'er to be with her ... to ... I finally talked her into it ... making love, if I hadn't begged her to ... if I just hadn't ... well, she might still be here today.

SABRINA. Excuse me?

DOUGLAS. That's how it happened, the heart attack! ... it was me, it was my fault, we were ... doing "it"!

SABRINA. I'm sorry, I must be missing something ... you were doing ... Oh, God, "it"! (*SHE suddenly laughs in spite of herself.*) Uh ... Douglas. Listen to me, this is one thing I know. If Connie had her way, and it sounds to me like she did ... she certainly would've wanted to ... uh, did, actually, go ... that way, with you, I mean. (*SHE turns to the coffin and winks.*)

DOUGLAS. You don't hate me ... you don't think ...

SABRINA. (*Shakes her head and hugs him.*) Trust me.

DOUGLAS. Mam?

SABRINA. Brina, please.

DOUGLAS. (*Feeling much better.*) Thank you. (*HE hesitates then kisses her.*) I'm really gonna miss her ... I'll leave you two alone. I know you probably have a lot to talk about. I'm glad to have met you.

SABRINA. And I you. Goodbye.

DOUGLAS. I don't like sayin' goodbye. I'll see ya. (*HE turns to leave.*)

SABRINA. My God, Con, what a way to go. Only you! He looks like James Dean in *East of Eden* ... And I was afraid you'd never really find him, that you'd never be happy and it would always truly be Michael. I'm glad you found him. I'm glad you let me know you found him. Now, we can both rest in peace. (*Pause.*) I was so damned happy when you called me last week. You sounded so ecstatic. (*SHE laughs.*) Now I know why!! I couldn't wait to see you. To hear your news. I wanted us to be as close as when we were kids. I wanted to sing "That's Amore" and eat garlic bread and drink Blue Nunn. I wanted to get in your '55 Chevy and drive through Steak 'N Shake. To go to Teen Town and dance to "Be Bop A Lula" and "Love Me Tender." I wanted us to go back to your room and play records on your Victrola and to hide behind your garage and smoke cigarettes and tell lies about all the boys we knew ... (*SHE runs her hand along the coffin.*) I wanted you to take me there, to make me laugh, just the way you always did. I was so happy, to know we were gonna take that trip together while we ate spaghetti and drank Blue Nun and Binky played "Volare."

ATTENDANT. (*Enters.*) I'm sorry. We do have to close up.

SABRINA. All right.

(*HE leaves.*)

SABRINA. He really does look like Al Pacino in *The Godfather*, Con, cross my heart ... God, I'm gonna miss you. I already do. Good ... See ya.

(As SHE exits we hear Connie's favorite song begin to play and we hear her voice as a PIN LIGHT comes up only on her face in the distance.)

CONNIE. So, Brin, don't be mad at me, okay? I know I was supposed to be at that Christmas domaggigy and that party for what's her name but I met this guy! He looks like a Greek God. Like Adonis or Hercules. Oh, I'm too old for him and you know what a sex maniac I am. As much as I'm dyin' to totally ravish his bod, I'm controlling myself. I'm crazy, I know, but I actually think this time I'm really in love. I'll tell you all about him when I see you. I can't wait to see you. Let's have spaghetti at Jimmy B's. We haven't been there in years. I'm dying to see if Stanley still has any of that beautiful curly hair ...

FADE TO BLACK

THE END

COSTUME LIST

SABRINA: Dress, wild and colorful, as if attending a party not a funeral. Simple pumps.

ATTENDANT: Simple dark suit, white shirt and tie, shoes and socks to match.

CONNIE:

High school scenes: Fifties Poodle skirt with crinolines, tight sweater, oxfords, bobby socks and scarf on her ponytail.

Duggie scene at train & following: Frilly prom dress, soft and pretty. Pump heels and gloves.

Jerry wedding: sixties, hippy style, fringe and boots, head band and long beads.

Michael/Maternity ward scene: straight skirt, late fifties, with simple blouse and oxfords/bobby socks.

Dr. Hausler/hospital scene: Frilly shortie pajamas under a chenille bathrobe.

Dr. Macon's office scene: Seventies, wild print or flowered dress, low heels and hat.

Sabrina/funeral scene: Simple dress, dark color, price tag hanging on zipper. Simple pumps and black bag, wearing glasses.

MICHAEL:

<u>High school & Duggie train scene</u>: Jeans, rolled up, white shirt and tee-shirt, loafer shoes.

<u>Jerry wedding</u>: Flowered sixties shirt and slacks.

<u>Maternity ward</u>: Blue jeans, loafers and short sleeve shirt.

<u>Funeral scene:</u> Polyester leisure suit, brown shoes and socks, white shirt and tie.

DUGGIE: Army uniform, dress khaki's, fifties.

JERRY: Motorcycle jacket, boots, head band – sixties.

DR. HAUSLER: Loud jacket, colored shirt and ascot, dark slacks and dress shoes with black socks.

DR. MACON: White lab coat, simple skirt and comfortable shoes.

CONNIE'S MOTHER: Shorts, flowered top, big straw hat and sandals.

CARRIE: Simple pastel dress with pumps

DOUGLAS: Army uniform, dress greens, eighties, with shoes, hat and rest to match.

NURSE: White nurses' uniform, with shoes and hose to match.

PRINCIPAL: Cardigan sweater, shirt, tie, jacket and slacks. shoes and socks to match.

PROPERTY LIST

Yellow roses bouquet – at coffin
A large shopping bag containing:
     A Dean Martin record album, and player
     A red-checkered tablecloth
     A bottle of white wine and two glasses
     Sabrina's purse, containing handkerchief, and cork
     screw

A basketball – Michael, first scene
Michael's glasses (three progressive changes as he ages)
Bubble gum
A frog or the appearance of one
Principal's file, ink pen & school books
Price tags, for Connie throughout and large tag on
     Connie's coffin.

A single yellow rose – (Duggie to Connie)
Duffel bag (Duggie)

Sun hat and sunglasses (Connie's mother)
Bubble gum - (Connie's mother)
Telephone receivers (2)

Head scarf and ring on neck chain (Connie)
Guitar
Motorcycle helmet
Wrist corsage

Magazines – fifties, sixties and eighties

Stethoscope and clipboard (Maternity ward nurse & Dr. Macon)

Pipe, ascot and file folder (Dr. Hausler)
Fuzzy house slippers (Connie)

A single yellow rose (Douglas to Sabrina)

MAIN SET, CENTER: Funeral Parlor should be
slightly elevated and remain in tact throughout.

Surrounding open stage area should change with
each scene and should be interspersed with
hanging, shreds of grey scrim to represent
Sabrina's mind/memories. All set pieces in
these scenes should also be grey or dark in color.
Costumes should be bright and very colorful.

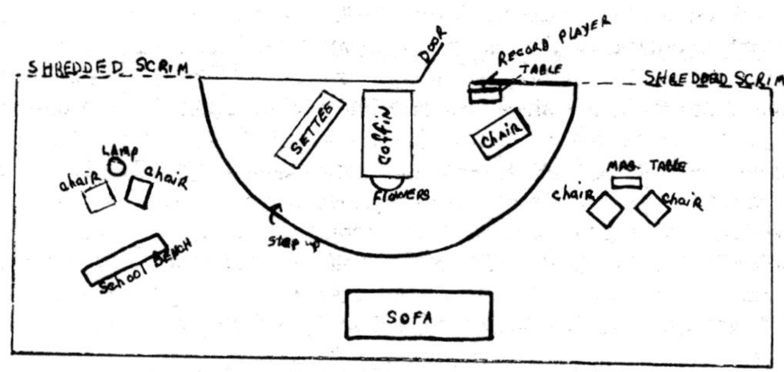

Center sofa scenes:
Connie in Hospital
Sabrina in Hospital
Sabrina's daughter's funeral

School bench: Highschool scene

Lamp & two chairs:
Wedding Chapel scene

Mag. Table/ two chairs:
Doctor's Office scene &
Connie & Michael in
Maternity waiting room.

Open staging with no set pieces at all should be used in
all other scenes so that actors can utilize the entire space,
the exception being, of course, all those scenes inside the
Main/Funeral Parlor set.

CEMENTVILLE
by Jane Martin
Comedy
Little Theatre

(5m., 9f.) Int. The comic sensation of the 1991 Humana Festival at the famed Actors Theatre of Louisville, this wildly funny new play by the mysterious author of *Talking With* and *Vital Signs* is a brilliant portrayal of America's fascination with fantasy entertainment, "the growth industry of the 90's." We are in a run-down locker room in a seedy sports arena in the Armpit of the Universe, "Cementville, Tennessee," with the scurviest bunch of professional wrasslers you ever saw. This is decidedly a small-time operation—not the big time you see on TV. The promoter, Bigman, also appears in the show. He and his brother Eddie are the only men, though; for the main attraction(s) are the "ladies." There's Tiger, who comes with a big drinking problem and a small dog; Dani, who comes with a large chip on her shoulder against Bigman, who owes all the girls several weeks' pay; Lessa, an ex-Olympic shotputter with delusions that she is actually employed presently in athletics; and Netty, an overweight older woman who appears in the ring dressed in baggy pajamas, with her hair in curlers, as the character "Pajama Mama." There is the eager-beaver go-fer Nola, a teenager who dreams of someday entering the glamorous world of pro wrestling herself. And then, there are the Knockout Sisters, refugees from the Big Time but banned from it for heavy-duty abuse of pharmaceuticals as well as having gotten arrested *in flagrante delicto* with the Mayor of Los Angeles. They have just gotten out of the slammer; but their indefatigable manager, Mother Crocker ("Of the Auto-Repair Crockers") hopes to get them reinstated, if she can keep them off the white powder. Bigman has hired the Knockout Sisters as tonight's main attraction, and the fur really flies along with the sparks when the other women find out about the Knockout Sisters. Bigman has really got his hands full tonight. He's gotta get the girls to tear each other up in the ring, not the locker room; he's gotta deal with tough-as-nails Mother Crocker; he's gotta keep an arena full of tanked-up rubes from tearing up the joint—and he's gotta solve the mystery of who bit off his brother Eddie's dick last night.   (#5580)

Other Publications For Your Interest

PICTURE OF DORIAN GRAY, THE. (Little Theatre.) Drama. Adapted by John Osborne from the novel by Oscar Wilde. 11m., 4f., plus extras. I Int. w/apron for other scenes. English playwright John Osborne (Look Back in Anger, Inadmissible Evidence, The Entertainer) has given us a brilliant dramatisation of Wilde's classic novel about a young man who, magically, retains his youth and beauty while the decay of advancing years and moral corruption only appears on a portrait painted by one of his lovers. Following the advice of the evil Lord Harry, a cynic who, fashionably, mocks any and all institutions and moral precepts, Dorian comes to believe that the only purpose of life is simply for one to realize, and glorify, one's own nature. In so doing, he is inevitably sucked into the maelstrom of degradation and despair, human nature being what it is. "Osborne has done much more than a scissors-and-paste job on Wilde's famous story. He has thinned out the over-abundant epigrams, he has highlighted the topical concept of youth as a commodity for which one would sell one's soul and he has, in Turn of the Screw fashion, created a sense of evil through implication. Osborne conveys moral disintegration through the gradual breakdown of the hero's language into terse, broken phrases and through a creeping phantasmagoria."—London, The Guardian. "What is so interesting about John Osborne's adaptation of The Picture of Dorian Gray is that he had found in Oscar Wilde's macabre morality a velveted barouche for his own favorite themes. Osborne funks none of the greenery-valley vulgarity of the fabulous story, and conveys much of its fascination."—London, Daily Telegraph. State author when ordering.   (#18954)

FALL OF THE HOUSE OF USHER, THE. (Little Theatre.) Drama. Gip Hoppe. Music by Jay Hagenbuckle. 6m. 3f. Int. A comfortable suburban family man receives a desperate telephone call from an obscure and forgotten childhood acquaintance. Thus starts a journey into madness that will take Ed Allen to the House of Usher and the terrible secrets and temptations contained there. In this modern adaptation of the classic short story by Edgar Allen Poe, playwright Gip Hoppe takes Gothic horror into the 90s, questioning the definition of "sanity" in the same way Poe did in his day. Ed arrives to find Roderick in a state of panic and anxiety over the impending death of his sister, Madeline. As he tries to sort out the facts, he becomes tangled in a family web of incest and murder. Finding himself infatuated with the beautiful Madeline, his "outside life" fades from his memory as he descends to the depths of madness that inflict all the residents of The House of Usher. *The Fall of the House of Usher* is an exhilarating theatrical adventure leading to an apocalyptic ending that will have audiences thrilled. Actors and designers will be challenged in new ways in this unpredictable and wildly entertaining play. Cassette tape. Use of Mr. Hagenbuckle's music will greatly enhance the play, but it is not mandatory.   (#7991)